# Sex, Abstinence and Happiness

By James Nugent

## Preface

What follows is a frank discussion about sexual behavior and the consequences of that behavior. It is an argument for saving sexual intercourse for marriage. This short book proposes abstinence as a radical solution to the problems inherent, in the now defunct sexual revolution.

## Disclaimer

This discussion is not in any way a substitute for professional counseling or psychotherapy. If you suspect you have these issues go to a competent professional to get help. This is just an adult discussion and nothing therapeutic is intended to come out of this booklet.

## About the Author James Nugent

My BA is in Criminal Justice and English Literature. My MA is in Counseling and Community Psychology. I was a counselor for 22 years in part time private practice. My full time work has been in Education and I hold teaching endorsements in Psychology, English Lit., Spanish and Special Education. I am a devout Roman Catholic. I dedicated the last 30 years to trying to make the world a better place.

Women are getting cheated.

Note

All names were changed and all identifying characteristic have been sanitized from this presentation. Any apparent connection between this book and real people and events is coincidental.

An estimated 25% of women, who are cohabitating, need professional mental health assistance at some time in their lives. The single most common complaint in my private practice was depression which appeared within a year of having an abortion. For two decades I helped women and men deal with the emotional strain put upon them by the life style choices they were making.

In the end most of my clients never changed their choices and so never really got much relief from their symptoms. It became clear, to me, that all of us make choices and suffer the consequences of those choices. It caused me to look outside the box for a cure for the pain and suffering I was seeing.

## Maybe We Need to Rethink the Sexual Revolution

Maybe there is something inherently unhealthy with the sexual revolution?  Maybe people should wait until marriage and when they want to have a baby?  Maybe people could have intensely pleasurable non-sexual relationships?  When I first mentioned that this might be possible to a colleague she just rolled her eyes.

The following week I was helping a 16 year old girl named Ashley. She had an abortion when she was 15 years old. She was suicidal. She wanted the love of a boyfriend but really didn't want to go through the emotional roller coaster of being pregnant and then having to decide on killing the child or raising him or her again.  She also resented being as she called it, "the sperm holder", waiting to find out if she was pregnant each month.

She recently went to Planned Parenthood and got: birth control pills, condoms and spermicide.  She was in emotional agony because there was still a 1/2% chance she would get pregnant again. She also had troublesome side effects from the pill. I asked her if she ever considered not having sex until she wanted a baby. She laughed and then thought about it. She quietly said that sex and boys really go together. I gently suggested that this wasn't necessarily true. I also suggested that a boy was not a man and a man should not ask a woman to risk her physical and financial future just because he wants to spray some sperm around. She left chuckling and thinking.

The next week she was happy. She said she had quite a long talk with her boyfriend. She told him it wasn't fair for her to risk everything for a boy who didn't even have a job! She broke up with him and she felt empowered and good. She mentioned she can have sex anytime she wants, but she was going to try it again when she is finished with her education. It turned out I was invited to her wedding 12 years later. She was a pediatrician and wanted to have one of her own children. The invitation had tiny pro-life feet on the back.


Ashely was a success story. Often it didn't go so well.

## An Argument for Abstinence

A whole lot of us are trying desperately and with gusto to be happy while failing miserably. We drag ourselves into counselor offices and doctor offices and in the end we are asking to have feelings that just don't go along with our daily sexual behavior.

It is kind of like the guy who kept hitting his hand with a hammer and then went to the doctor repeatedly asking for pain pills. The point is that if you want the pain to go away you must stop doing the thing that causes you so much pain.

## Sex is not bad

Sex is not a bad thing. Beyond the fact that it can be exquisitely pleasurable it serves at least two more purposes. It promotes pair bonding and child bearing. When we try to separate out these very powerful primitive and hormonally based purposes from the pleasure aspect; it is there we seem to get into trouble.

No matter how good the sex, if it is with a person with whom we don't have a committed relationship; we are in the end lonely. Even if we agree together that this it is just a purely physical relationship, we still want something more out of life.

We still want that basic human need for belonging and love to be filled. If a person convinces themselves, that they don't need love; they have enough material for years of therapy. It just isn't true.

Then the issue of conception raises its head! Not every woman wants to bear children. Not every woman wants to bear a child at various times in their life span. No method of contraception is 100% effective and some have dangerous side effects.

The Pill is Poison

The World Health Organization has recently stated that the pill is a Class I carcinogen. Agencies around the world now concede that the water tables are polluted with this carcinogen. Yet in an attempt to have the pleasure and or the bonding while avoiding conception; women ingest this poison every day. It makes more sense to abstain from recreational sexual intercourse until the time and partner are right.

## Other Hazards of Promiscuity

Twenty percent of us have herpes. Many of the sexually transmitted diseases of the past are superbugs today, and resistant to antibiotics now.  Doctors had to change the term "safe sex" into "safer sex" because condoms, dental dams and latex gloves don't provide perfect protection. They are more like 75% effective in real life usage. The penalty for having casual sex can easily mean life-long injury or death. It kind of takes the fun out of the whole activity if you think about it.

## Emotional Injury

This is the area in which I spent two decades. Many of my clients were very unhappy because of the choices they were making in the lives.  They were often unwilling to make changes yet wanted symptom relief. Some of the emotional pains were very serious indeed. Anxiety and depression were the most common and can be debilitating or fatal. Some of my clients were heavily medicated by their doctors but still unwilling to even look at what might be the cause of this misery.

## Boys and Girls Just Want to Have Fun

These are people who will give away intimacy and keep trying to tell themselves sex without commitment is just fun. They try to protect themselves from being hurt by not caring about the intimate sexual behavior. The reasoning is that if you don't care, then what is the harm in a little athletic sex? Isn't sex just a pleasurable past time, a leisure time activity?

Men have it easier. Except for fears of sexually transmitted disease or the powerlessness trauma of a sex partner going off and having an abortion; men have it easier. Men can deny that they need love and belonging, and use women at will. No wonder so many women hate men. Men risk little and can have a good time. The women are left poisoning their bodies with the pill and as my 16 year old client said so elegantly, "Holding the sperm."

The pill was supposed to make women carefree just like men seem to be when it comes to sexual intimacy, but it didn't. It just made it a little easier to be in denial.

What of Men's Issues?

I only counseled with a few men on sexually related issues but two clients come to mind. The first man was in his 20's and devastated by catching herpes. He felt like he was "damaged goods" and nobody would ever love him. He was suffering acute depression and loneliness. Using a reality therapy approach, and his personal physician for medicating the depression, he did recover. He checked in by phone 2 years later and told me he was getting married. The woman had caught herpes years before and felt better having a husband who had it too. He also mentioned that they had not had sex yet and were saving it for their wedding night. The radical idea abstinence had come to him on his own. He said he decided it is mean, to just use women, even if they wanted to be used.

The other man I counseled had been quite the exploiter of young women in his youth. Ten years before, he actually got two different girls pregnant in a 2 month time period, in his senior year of high school. He was now suffering acute guilt. Night and day he was claimed to be obsessing on his past. I was never really sure if he really felt guilt or was just using that as a narcissistic ploy to get me to help him with the Court.

Girl number one sued him for child support then got his parental rights dismissed because he was physically abusive on five occasions. He did jail time for some of the assaults. He said he has changed and longs to see his old girlfriend. I explained that since his ex was now married and had more children; she might not want him in her life. Maybe, just maybe it was okay for him to move on.


Girl number two had quietly and quickly had an abortion and moved to Montana. This sincerely hurt him. He went through a deep grieving process which still wasn't finished a decade later. He participated vigorously in grief counseling with me and found relief. It never occurred to me before, that men could be hurt by abortion too. It turns out that some men grieve the death of their offspring.


The Burdens Women Carry

So men and women are different. One the falsehoods of the sexual revolution is that if women can freely engage with multiple sex partners she will feel free like men seem to feel.

However, because women conceive and bear children; they feel differently about sexual relationships.

This does not make women inferior to men. It just makes them different. With nearly half our marriages ending in divorce we need to take a look at how men and women do intimacy and perhaps make some culture wide changes. If we don't rethink the sexual revolution things will continue to get worse.

Recent research into male promiscuity has consistently found that most men will cheat on a mate or spouse when tempted. One study found that all the married males in the study were willing to have sex with another woman if there was no chance of being caught. This should not surprise women. They have noted that men will lie and cheat in order to have sex. Single women often just accept lying as part of the whole mating ritual.

The most common issue in failed marriages is finances. The most common major expense is children. Should married women just buck up and take their poison pills? No, there is a better pro-life way.

Modern Natural Family Planning is non-toxic and in a recent study of 30,000 couples found that it is just as effective as the pill.

Natural Family Planning (NFP) uses the monitoring of basic body symptoms to identify when a women is fertile. If a couple doesn't want a baby they just abstain from sex for a few days.

Intermittent Abstinence in Marriage?

Yes.  A couple can cuddle and talk and build a relationship. When it is time to continue sexual relations it is just an extension of the loving and caring partnership that they have. Gasp!:>  One angry colleague told me once that she didn't get married to abstain from sex.

In the seventh year of her over sexualized relationship she admitted that you can be naked and married and still not have an intimately rewarding relationship. Her marriage failure was not caused by a lack of the sex but rather caused by the lack of intimacy.

Intimacy

Somebody taught me a long time ago that intimacy literally means "In-to-me-see."  Intimacy means to look into the very personality of another human being. As the observer we must must be respectful and caring. Another word for personality might be soul. It is the collection of thoughts, feelings and habits of choice that make up the real person behind the naked body. It is the part of a person that we love and by which we are loved. When we are intimate with another person's soul, it can be a joyful and ecstatic event. It is love and it is related to but not dependent on sex.

When we separate sex from intimacy (Love) and commitment we exploit the other person for our own pleasure. When two people are willing to exploit each other for their own pleasure, it is very shaky ground for a marriage or any long term relationship.

The human need for love and belonging is probably written into our genetic code. If we frustrate it by settling for something less, we are vulnerable to all sorts of neurosis and misery. When perceived as an unmet need, this need can drive us to all sorts of creative and unhealthy solutions to the problem. Men unable to achieve intimacy in their own marriages look around for other sexual conquests. They misunderstand that it is the bonding found in the intimacy with a life-long spouse that can really satisfy that burning desire.

Men and women must change their perspectives. Men must see that a woman is much more that a vagina. Women must see that a man is much more than a penis. I suspect that it is easier for a woman to change than a man because women suffer more because of the sexual revolution. A man's perspective is much more resistant to change because he suffers less, although he does suffer. But let me be clear, sex without love (intimacy) and commitment makes everyone unhappy.

Only a good dose of empathy and compassion will shake a man out of the exploitative attitude that is running amuck in our society.

If I Had My Way

If I could restructure our culture, this is what I would do. Parents would teach their children respectful loving relationships long before an interest in sex arises. Little boys and girls would empathize and have joyful friendships.

Teens would then have multiple cross gender relationships that would satisfy their growing need for intimacy and emancipation. It would be generally unthinkable for a teen boy to lie to a teen girl in order to exploit her for sex. The same would be for teen girls.

There would be three levels of proactive defense against teen pregnancy. The boy and the girl would see the practical benefits of waiting for marriage. Teen girls would not want to risk their physical, mental, and academic futures for sex. Society would have a taboo on pre-marital sex. This is not too far-fetched. Half the high school seniors are sexually abstinent now and it is not because sex is not available.

Separating pleasure from intimacy and commitment has caused this social mess we are in right now. Anything that promotes more of the same is counterproductive.

So the problem is not more sex and better birth control. We need more and better programs that enhance self-esteem and empathy in boys and girls, and men and women. Until people respect and care for themselves and the people around them; the battle between the sexes which was exacerbated by the pill will continue. The misery inside and outside of marriage caused by our sexual behavior will continue. Divorce will continue to be epidemic.

Talking About Sex and Sexuality

One of the problems in contemporary society has been the general inability to discuss sexual relationships. We have delegated the discussion to the public schools and mostly that is a discussion about biology. While biology is important information it does not cover discussions on intimacy and values and relationships.

In all fairness to the schools they are pretty much forbidden to discuss values. Therefore they contribute to the downfall of society which is dying at its roots because we have separated intimacy from sexual behavior. Recently an award winning teacher in Oregon was so frustrated by this issue, that he threw Planned Parenthood out of his classroom. He was fired.

We must discuss sexual relationships in our homes, churches, and youth organizations. The Girl Scouts have been discussing sexuality in the USA for years. The problem is that it has been a discussion based on biology, not respectful intimacy and relationships.   This just makes the whole issue worse.

While churches have been hesitant to open this whole can of worms there is some hint that prudishness is going out of fashion. Some Youth Groups in Roman Catholic Parishes have been discussing abstinence as an alternative to perils and pleasures of premarital sexual activity. I asked a counseling client what she got out of one of these presentations. She said she learned that she was important enough to wait until marriage before she has sex. Any boy who doesn't understand that isn't worth her time. I wish I had been at the presentation but there is hope for a better society if young women think more highly of themselves and think their futures worthy of protecting.


The problem is much more involved than teaching young women to say "no." It is just as important to teach young men to not participate in the predatory sexual exploitation of young women. Teach them sexuality is not a game to be played for fun and sport. There is a person behind that body who longs for love and belonging too. Someday she may find a partner and then decide to have children. Lying and cheating in order to get sex makes you less of person.

Of course there are women who have bought into the whole sexual revolution and want to treat men in the rather exploitive way in which women have been treated. I say good luck with that as you wait to find out if this is the month you are pregnant. Research consistently shows that a whole lot of you will be seen in counselor's offices or the doctor's office for stress related issues because of your relationships.

The cure for all this stress is, don't have sexual intercourse unless you are at least willing to consider having a baby.

Catholics have a line in the marriage sacrament that asks the couple, "Are you willing to accept children?" This is a brilliant idea. If both partners are willing to have children there will be less strife and anguish in the bedroom! To the degree that each person is telling the truth; sex will be an integrated experience of pleasure, and commitment. Sex can be a sharing of souls not just a rubbing together of bodies like dogs humping on the side of the road.

By now with an understanding of what I mean by real intimacy; you may realize that this attitude could change everything you think, do and feel in the privacy of your own sex life.

 Some of you will not understand because you don't want to understand. Some of you acutely fear change. Others are just committed to hedonism and will see no need to change. Some of you will be angry because you perceive a threat to your sexual pleasures. All of that is really beside the point.

Happiness

You cannot be happy unless your behavior has a real chance at getting you what you really want.  If you want belonging and love and your actions are to the contrary; you will not be happy. The standard answer of a man or woman who involved in sexual activity outside marriage may be that they don't want commitment, only physical pleasure. If it weren't for the possibility of women getting pregnant because they retain the sperm and wait; this might be possible.

Alas every sexually active woman has to deal with this possibility every month. The other issue which is unstoppable is every normal human being needs love and a sense of belonging.

A Suggestion

Try an experiment. Set aside a specific period of time where you will try building non-sexual yet intimate friendships with the opposite sex. Maybe it will be six months or a year. Learn to appreciate who they are and learn about their hopes and dreams. Share your hopes and dreams. Be intimate. If the subject comes up feel free to discuss your experiment in abstinence.

When the trial period ends, examine the relationships you have. Take a good look at the quality of your non-sexual relationships. You will find that they have a quality that surpasses your sexual relationships. It is a quality that is born of respectfully sharing. It can be intensely pleasurable. You may find it longer lasting and more rewarding than your last orgasm.

It is from these non-sexual non-exploitive relationships you might even find love and possibly life-long commitment.

James Nugent 2013

Other Books by James Nugent

How I Sailed From Olympia to The San Juan Islands, and Returned Safely

An Alternative Boating Guide to Southern Puget Sound

How and Why I lived Aboard

Kayaking Budd Inlet in South Puget Sound

I Speak Esperanto

The Rainbow Road and Other Signs of God's Love

Living an Abundant Life, Within Your Means

Social Jujitsu and Powerful Principles for Managing Social Conflict

Blackjack on My Small Budget

A Little Benedictine Oblate Manuel

Without Speech

All Things Work

Loving Time with Your Creator

Personal Adventures in a Life of Learning

The Good News about Being Catholic

E-book Writing and Overcoming Barriers to Creativity

E-book Writing and Organizing Your Ideas

My Forty Days For Life 2013

Lifestyle Realty Observing

How to Sail in the Winter

How to Get Your Kid to Move Out

*Available at Amazon.com in Kindle E-Book and or Audible Book or Paperback*

## Sex, Abstinence and Happiness

# Sex, Abstinence and Happiness

www.ingramcontent.com/pod-product-compliance
Lightning Source LLC
Chambersburg PA
CBHW060352290526
45791CB00004B/1649

* 9 7 8 1 4 9 4 7 4 6 2 6 1 *